COLORS OF IMA

Colors of Ima
A True Story About My Friendship With Horses
Copyright © 2021 by Christine Perry
Illustrated by Karin Ferro

Additional copies may be ordered from the publisher for educational, business,
promotional or premium use. For information, contact ALIVE Book Publishing at:
alivebookpublishing.com, or call (925) 837-7303.

Book Design by Alex P. Johnson

ISBN 13
978-1-63132-144-3 Hardback

Library of Congress Control Number: 2021913675

Library of Congress Cataloging-in-Publication Data is available upon request.

First Edition

Published in the United States of America by ALIVE Book Publishing
and ALIVE Publishing Group, imprints of Advanced Publishing LLC
3200 A Danville Blvd., Suite 204, Alamo, California 94507
alivebookpublishing.com

PRINTED IN THE UNITED STATES OF AMERICA

10 9 8 7 6 5 4 3 2 1

COLORS OF IMA

A True Story About My Friendship With Horses

Written by Christine Perry
Illustrated by Karin Ferro

ABOOKS
Alive Book Publishing

This book is dedicated to the loves of my life,
Fawshi and Rosie,
whose enduring friendships have enhanced my life so much.
They have taught me about love, patience, commitment,
trust, and to always believe in the possible.

Acknowledgements

I want to thank all the people who showed me the way with my horses and helpd me along the trails of life. To my mom, Susan Perry, Lynn Palm, and Cyril Pittion-Rossillon— your words and ways of training that you demonstrated over the years are always with me!

I also thank Michele Ulrech, Linda Gubanski, Ray Hunt, Sharon Camarillo, Jim Hunter, and my many friends at Summit Ranch in Alamo, California. The wonderful life friendships and connections are too long to name; to an incredible community, near and far, I offer a huge, heartfelt, thank you.

Ima Star Watcher is a beautiful brown
American Quarter Horse
with hind white socks on her legs,
white markings on her face,
and a black mane and tail.
Her "Barn Name"—what we call her— is Ima.

Ima's coloring is known as "Bay."

Susan, Ima's owner, was excited for Ima to have a foal.
She hoped Ima would have a splashy "paint horse."

O A Paint Horse is one with two inches of white
somewhere on the body besides the legs and face.
O The term "splashy in color" means
a lot of white coloring on the horse.

Ima was a smart horse.
She could hear cars coming up the road to the stable,
and was always happy to see people.
Ima liked certain visitors, just like people do.

At the age of three, it was time to choose the sire horse
for the best paint coloring, body confirmation,
and good personality.

○ It takes about eleven days short of a year for a foal to be born.
○ Sire is the dad.

One cool February morning,
Ima gave birth to a magical stud (male) colt.
Both Susan and Ima were proud of this cute little colt.
He was a stallion with a lot of white paint.
The new baby foal's registered name was
Socket Stars-n-Stripes. His barn name is Socks.

Socks was such a beautiful example of what an
American Paint Horse should look like,
with his chestnut and white coloring.
He had beautiful, kind, expressive, dark eyes.

Chestnut is a warm red-gold brown color.

Regional Paint Horse Show

Socks grew up to become a big, strong, reliable show
horse. He was a handsome horse to ride, and a perfect
gentleman in the barn. His charming personality made
him popular with his trainers, barn visitors, and friends.

Socks liked donuts as a treat.
Most Saturday mornings, Susan would greet him
at his stall with a big glazed donut or two!

Years later, Ima had another foal.
This time a filly (female) was born.

She looked just like her mom,
with brown and white facial markings,
and four white socks.

The brand new foal was beautiful,
but she was not considered a paint horse, because
she did not have white markings on her body.

When the new foal was three days old,
Susan's daughter, Christine, decided to
visit Ima and her new baby.

When Christine got out of the car,
this new baby foal ran straight over
and into Christine's arms!
This foal was not afraid of a thing.

The baby pranced around in circles,
wanting to play. Her momma was not amused at this,
and reared up into the air, as if to say, "Get over here!"

Ima taught her new baby foals everything
by talking to them. She would whinny directions,
telling her young ones where to go
and what they could feel safe with.

Ima communicated with her ears.
"Ears up" meant *alert* or *okay*, while "ears back" was warning:
Mom does not like what you are doing!

One day it was shower time, and Ima's baby learned to be
comfortable in the wash rack, right alongside her mom.

The new filly (girl) soon became Christine's horse,
given as a gift from her mother, Susan. Christine and the
filly loved each other from the moment they met.

Christine named her "Fashion Emergency," and
at the barn we called her *Fawshi*.

As Fawshi continued to grow, so did her beauty.
She became a show horse, as well as Christine's companion.

Fawshi won her first two horse shows in her yearling year.
She loves audiences, applause,
and most of all, she loves people!

Fawshi is a show off!

She had her own birthday party at the age of one,
at the boarding stable where she lived.

People came from near and far to see her
run free in the arena. She ran as fast as she could,
showing off for her guests.

People at the party enjoyed carrot cake,
while all the horses in the barn
munched on carrots to celebrate!
Everyone took pictures and played games.

*Even though a horse has a true birthday, according to
breeds' registration, horses are considered a year
older on January first,
regardless of their actual birth date.*

Now it was Ima's turn to learn how to become
a riding horse. She did not love it at first,
but learned to trust the rider on her back.
This gave her a better life with people.

Ima loved attention. When she was out in a pasture
without people around, she missed
the attention of being groomed and exercised.

Ima also liked dogs, and the chicken
that would sleep on her back
when she was in her stall!

Then it was time for Fawshi to learn to be a riding horse.
Her trainer, Michele, got her used to having a saddle on her back.
Fawshi became a beautiful riding horse.
She enjoys horse shows, and going to clinics to learn new skills.
Trail riding on the mountain
is one of her favorite things to do.

Fawshi was growing up fast,
and loved to run, run, and run!

Fawshi and Christine would hike up Mt. Diablo,
through the cows, water, tall grass, and rocks.
It was on the mountain that Fawshi grew accustomed to bikes,
joggers, hikers, coyotes, and squirrels.

These trips taught her to trust Christine.
Often, if Christine would touch something,
Fawshi would calmly check it out and not be afraid.

Ima was due to have another foal by the same sire as Socks,
but this time, she had a beautiful black filly,
with four white socks and a blaze.

This beautiful foal's was named "Ima Cutie Patootie."
We called her "Rosie," at the barn.

Rosie did not come out as a paint horse,
but she was beautiful!
Rosie and Fawshi are both known as
Paints that Ain't.

After a few months, Rosie injured her
legs from running so hard at such a young age.

Every day, she needed twenty minutes of hand walking
along side her mom, before she could frolic freely.

Rosie was so beautiful and friendly,
she soon became a favorite at the barn.

Happy to be brushed, she would lean on who was brushing her,
hoping they would never stop. She loved taking baths,
closing her eyes and letting the water run over her.

Christine fell in love with Rosie while caring for her
all the time. Christine bought Rosie,
and kept her at the stable with her half sister, Fawshi.

Fawshi and Rosie love each other.
They have separate stalls to live in, but enjoy being
turned out together for play time and relaxation.

Rosie also won her yearling horse show,
for her beauty and good manners.

Rosie and Fawhsi are both good horses,
but Rosie was harder to train. She kicked out
with both back legs when she was scared
or did not like something.

She was spooked by many things.
Rosie would whirl around,
or leap in the air at any moment.

Rosie was always a bit scared,
and this caused Christine to fall off three times.

She would spin around really fast, and off Christine went
to the ground. But Rosie was very cute about it.
Whenever she felt Christine fall off, she would stop and
look at Christine, as if to say,
"What are you doing down there?"

Rosie likes it when a rider squeezes gently to assure her,
with both hands and legs, just like a big hug!

Once Christine understood this,
they became good partners in the show arena.

Socks, Fawshi, and Rosie have been
riding nicely for some time, having many experiences.

A famous horse trainer, Lynn Palm, once trained
all three, as student horses in a demonstration
with Christine, at the Sacramento Horse Expo.

Lynn would ride all the horses, and guide
Christine with new skills for riding quietly and skillfully.

People came to learn how to be better riders.
They learned how to direct their horses where to go
and at what speed to go, smoothly.
Riders learned how to have their horse:
- Walk
- Trot
- Canter (gallop)
- Stop
- Back-up

This process of classic riding makes both horse
and rider happy and comfortable.

Christine rode Fawshi without a bridle,
to demonstrate how to have soft hands while riding.
Fawshi was so beautiful and smooth
without a bridle, and she really liked it!

"Bridleless" is for arena riding, to demonstrate
how a rider uses their seat and legs,
along with gentle guidance of a rope around the horse's
neck for direction, with nothing in the horse's mouth.

Then it was time for Ima to have another foal.
This time, Susan decided to have Ima go to a
special foaling center.

This was a wise choice, because the foal's birth was different.
The umbilical cord broke, and the ranch owner,
Sharon, was right there to assist, clearing the foal's
mouth and nose so she could breathe.

The foal could have died, but luckily, didn't.
She is a beautiful *Paint!*

The new, beautiful foal's name is "Sunset Kisses."
Her barn name is Grace.
Ima and Grace made a beautiful pair
in the field, together for six months before weaning.
Grace was stunning but sassy,
and sometimes she was too much to handle.
As she frolicked in the pasture with Ima,
it was clear that she was beautiful and bold in every way.

As Grace grew up healthy and strong,
it was decided that Ima would stop having foals.
Ima would be turned out in fields, to be ridden sometimes,
but mainly just to relax and enjoy life.

Grace needed a lot of training at a slow pace.
Once she was safe for Christine to ride,
we brought her home to our barn.
Now all of Ima's babies were trained and riding.
Grace was different.

Weaning means to separate mom and foal.

She wanted all Christine's attention at the barn.
But Christine could not give Grace the attention
that she wanted. Even after a long ride,
she would demand by whinnying, pacing, and pawing.
She did not like being turned out in a paddock.
Grace wanted to be with Christine.

Christine met Dr. Dan. He wanted a horse to love.
"I think I have the horse for you," she told him.
Upon first meeting, Dr. Dan and Grace were quite a pair.
At first, Christine did not like the idea of selling Grace.
Grace was a beautiful paint that Christine had always wanted.
But selling Grace to Dr. Dan was the best thing to do for Grace.
Grace remained at the barn, and
Christine can still see her every day.
She now has a handsome owner who loves her.
Grace trusts him, and gallops through the hills,
enjoying trail riding with her man.
Grace still whinnies for Christine,
but only if Dr. Dan is not there.

As you can see, every horse has its own color
and personality, just like people!

When you are with horses, it is amazing
to see their little or big ways, and how they
show us their likes and dislikes.

The relationship between horses and people
is an amazing thing to experience.

I hope you can experience a horse soon.
Go to a local barn, introduce yourself and just watch.

It may be just a visit

or

it may be a trip of a lifetime of loving horses!

Either way, it is always a good day
when you are with horses!

Happy Trails

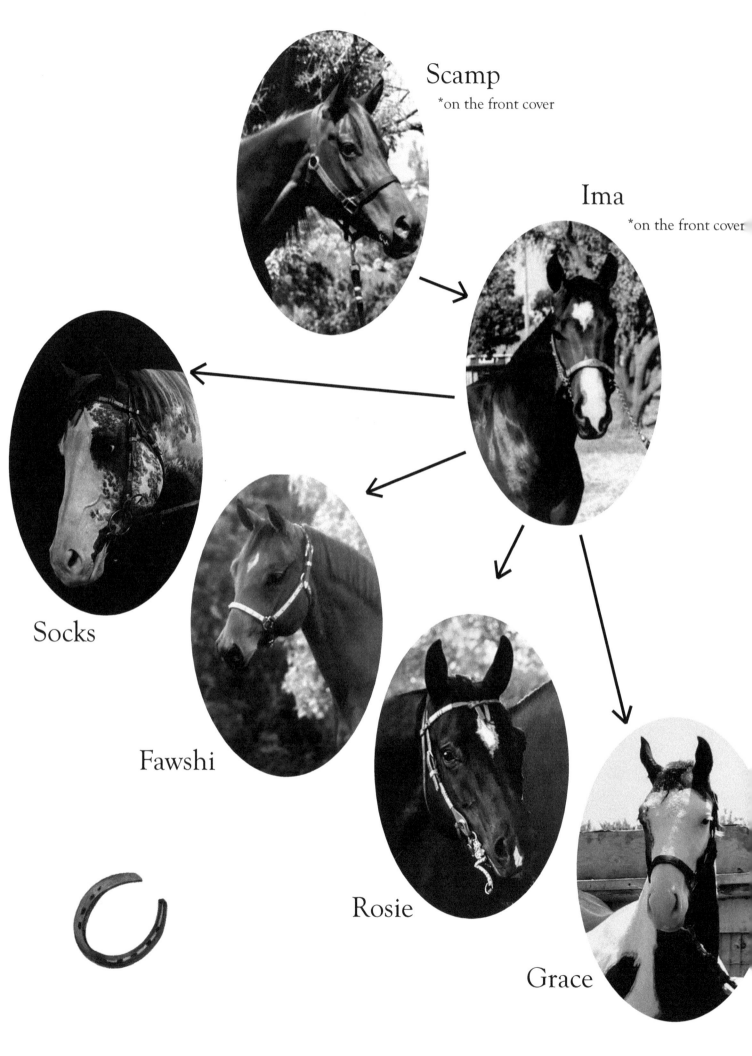

Scamp
*on the front cover

Ima
*on the front cover

Socks

Fawshi

Rosie

Grace

Christine Perry was born and raised in California's San Francisco Bay Area. Horses have been one of her life's passions. She believes that one is "never done learning to be a better horse rider," or as her trainer says, "You spend a lifetime learning to be light with your hands." As a hairstylist and salon owner for over thirty years, her clients' curiosity about horses inspired her to write this story.

Karin Ferro is an artist, illustrator, and watercolorist. She teaches art at a private school in the San Francisco Bay Area, and enjoys inspiring new artists. Karin graduated from Cal Poly in San Luis Obispo where she studied art. Karin has always had a love for painting animals and nature. In "The Colors of Ima," she captures the gentle, playful spirit of these wonderful animals.

ABOOKS

ALIVE Book Publishing and ALIVE Publishing Group
are imprints of Advanced Publishing LLC,
3200 A Danville Blvd., Suite 204, Alamo, California 94507

Telephone: 925.837.7303
alivebookpublishing.com

CPSIA information can be obtained
at www.ICGtesting.com
Printed in the USA
BVHW021418181121
621926BV00003B/114